RECEIVING AND EXERCISING THE AUTHORITY OF GOD

Retreat Leader Guide

WORKBOOK

RICHARD T. CASE

Dedication/Acknowledgements

I wish to dedicate this course to and thank my wife, Linda, and our ministry leaders who have learned how to step into and be exercising the authority available to us. This aspect of the Christian life is so misunderstood and certainly underutilized; typically Christians live in the "natural" focusing on cause & effect and logic to maneuver through life—and thus experience many difficulties that become "normal". There is a desire to follow Christian principles but the focus is on us doing the right things without regard to the power of God to overcome and change circumstances because of His authority over the natural (which was created by the Spiritual when He spoke all things into existence by His Word; and so the material, our circumstances are subordinate to His authority). Linda and the leaders have spent time in the Word and practicing that God hands this authority to us and we join Him in bringing supernatural power to our life. It is truly remarkable to experience this and realize the privilege we all have to receive and exercise His authority in real circumstances. Thank you Linda and ministry team for having hearts to follow, learn and then live out this most important aspect of Christian life as it was meant to be.

These leaders are:
Jake & Mary Beckel
Joe & Leigh Bogar
Heath & Rebecca Cardie
Rich & Janet Cocchiaro
Larry & Sherry Collett
Scott & Kristen Cornell
David & Melissa Dunkel
Tom & Susanne Ewing
Rick & Kelly Ferris
Joel & Christina Gunn
Scott & Terry Hitchcock
Rick & Nancy Hoover
Tad & Monica Jones
Ed & Becky Kobel
Don & Rachelle Light
Chris & Heidi May
Terry & Josephine Noetzel
Towanda Norton
Steve & Carolyn Van Ooteghem
Preston & Lynda Pitts
Dan & Kathy Rocconi
Bob & Keri Rockwell
John & Michelle Santaferraro
Allyson & Denny Weinberg
Neal & Kathy Weisenburger

LIVING IN AMAZING GRACE—THE NATURE OF GOD
PUBLISHED BY LIVING WATERS—ABIDE MINISTRIES
7615 Lemon Gulch Way
Castle Rock, CO 80108

Unless otherwise noted, all Scripture quotations are from the ESV® Bible (The Holy Bible, English Standard Version®), copyright © 2001 by Crossway Bibles, a publishing ministry of Good News Publishers. Used by permission. All rights reserved.

ISBN: 979-8-218-17375-3
Copyright © 2024 by Richard T. Case.

Publisher's Cataloging-in-Publication data

Names:
Title:
Description: .
Identifiers: ISBN | LCCN
Subjects:

Printed in the United States of America 2024 — 2nd ed

TABLE OF CONTENTS

LESSON 1:
WHAT IS THE AUTHORITY AND SUPERNATURAL WORK OF GOD?

As we start this new course, *Receiving and Exercising the Authority of God*, the authority that comes from God to us, we're going to explore something that's not widely known or appreciated in the Christian circles because it's not really talked about much. The thought primarily is: God has the authority, and we just pray that He exercises it. We hope He does. Sometimes He does. Sometimes He doesn't. We see that the world isn't getting any better, so we figure that He's certainly not making that happen. How do we explain this, particularly as we look at a world that is wicked, that is difficult. The underlying question is: How come God allows all that? We are called to understand God's authority, our role in that, and what happened that Satan wound up with authority over the world? How does that compare to God's authority? What role do we play in all this, and how do we exercise and experience this? Let's first look from scripture how authority is defined. The words interchangeably are: authority, dominion, ruling, power. You'll see these words throughout this study, and all have the same meaning. This refers to the splendor, majesty, beauty of God—the glory of Him, who has ultimate jurisdiction over the world and life, and has the power to cause things to change—to become great (much, many, and large, exceedingly abundant). He has the power to do the supernatural in the physical and in the spiritual realm, the right to govern, rulership, commanding and possessing authority. It's mighty work, strength, miraculous, performing miracles—the spectacular, the excellent.

From this scripture, write the basis for which God created all things. What does this mean regarding His authority, and why is this important to us?

> **Read Genesis 1:1–3:**
>
> The Creation of the World
> **1** In the beginning, God created the heavens and the earth. ² The earth was without form and void, and darkness was over the face of the deep. And the Spirit of God was hovering over the face of the waters.
>
> ³ And God said, "Let there be light," and there was light.

____

____

____

____

____

In the beginning of creation, He said: Let there be. And there was. So, His authority created what? Heaven and earth. He spoke it out of His power—He can speak His word into physical existence. That's amazing authority. The material, the circumstances, the things that we're involved with in this life are subordinated to what? His authority. He can spiritually speak something and change something. Why? He created it that way. It's subordinated and inferior to that, which makes it easier for us to understand. He created all with and by His authority, and all is under His authority.

What does "We are created in His image" mean? To whom did God give His authority? Why is this so significant as we understand how life on Earth was intended? What then was our role to be? Why?

> **Read Genesis 1:26:**
>
> 26 Then God said, "Let us make man[a] in our image, after our likeness. And let them have dominion over the fish of the sea and over the birds of the heavens and over the livestock and over all the earth and over every creeping thing that creeps on the earth."

____

____

____

____

____

He created us by speaking, and we are made in His image, which includes exercising His authority by speaking His spiritual words that changes things. We are reflecting God, the characteristics of God, including the power of God with us. And remember: We are the physical expression of the invisible God. So, God is including each of us in this authority, and we, men and women who are true followers of God, have authority over the Earth because we are superior to everything on Earth. Why are we superior to everything on Earth? Because we're created in His image, we have the essence of God within us. Do animals have that? No. It is true that animals have characteristics with superb abilities that are superior to us—but they don't rule us. We rule them. And we were intended to be that way. So, man and woman are the connectivity of the authority.

In the following two sets of verses, how do they describe God's Kingdom and His dominion (authority)? Why is this so significant to what life is available to us?

Read Daniel 4:34–35:

Nebuchadnezzar Restored

34 At the end of the days I, Nebuchadnezzar, lifted my eyes to heaven, and my reason returned to me, and I blessed the Most High, and praised and honored him who lives forever,

for his dominion is an everlasting dominion,
    and his kingdom endures from generation to generation;
35 all the inhabitants of the earth are accounted as nothing,
    and he does according to his will among the host of heaven
    and among the inhabitants of the earth;
and none can stay his hand
    or say to him, "What have you done?"

____

____

____

____

____

God's Kingdom and authority are everlasting—into eternity. It always has been and always will be everlasting. And the experience of that will be from generation to generation. It'll just keep going on and on and on. Physically, in our lifetime and the next lifetime and the next lifetime, His Kingdom, dominion, and authority still exist, and He reigns.

LESSON 1:
WHAT IS THE AUTHORITY AND SUPERNATURAL WORK OF GOD?

Read Jude 24–25:

Doxology

[24] Now to him who is able to keep you from stumbling and to present you blameless before the presence of his glory with great joy, [25] to the only God, our Savior, through Jesus Christ our Lord, be glory, majesty, dominion, and authority, before all time[a] and now and forever. Amen.

____

____

____

____

____

All majesty, all dominion, all authority are in Him—for the purpose that we might have joy in experiencing His splendor. So, the purpose of His authority is to reflect Himself. Who's the physical representation of Him? We are. So, we're involved in that dominion and authority because the purpose of it is to reflect Himself by us reflecting Him. If we're going to reflect Him, then we must be a participant and purveyor of that authority. We tend to think: Well, God's out there. Let's pray to Him. He's all powerful. Yes, to the omniscient, omnipotent God. Ask Him to take care of our life issues. However, He says: I'm doing this through you. You've got to be a player in this. What is your role? You're representing and reflecting the invisible God, which includes what? Authority.

How is this authority to be demonstrated and reflected? What does that mean for how we are to live out His life here on Earth? Why?

Read Psalm 45:8–14:

8   your robes are all fragrant with myrrh and aloes and cassia.
From ivory palaces stringed instruments make you glad;
9   daughters of kings are among your ladies of honor;
   at your right hand stands the queen in gold of Ophir.
10 Hear, O daughter, and consider, and incline your ear:
   forget your people and your father's house,
11   and the king will desire your beauty.
Since he is your lord, bow to him.
12   The people[a] of Tyre will seek your favor with gifts,
   the richest of the people.[b]
13 All glorious is the princess in her chamber, with robes interwoven with gold.
14   In many-colored robes she is led to the king,
   with her virgin companions following behind her.

____

____

____

____

____

He says His majesty and wondrous things will be reflected through what? You. By Him performing what? All kinds of miraculous things. It has to happen in reality within our real physical life. The miraculous is the nature of God, the authority of God. It was always to be. Had Adam and Eve not fallen and we, their offspring, stayed in a perfect world, would we have experienced the miraculous? Yes, because the miraculous isn't just about solving problems, but it is easy to demonstrate because of the problems. The authority and the miraculous is always here and is reflected through us exercising and experiencing His authority. He will become known to others around us as they see that His life through us is superior to the material.

LESSON 1:
WHAT IS THE AUTHORITY AND SUPERNATURAL WORK OF GOD?

From the following two sets of verses, what are the exceptional elements of what life intended for followers of God to live out? Why is this so significant to the definition of the life we are now to live out?

> **Read Genesis 1:26–31:**
>
> [26] Then God said, "Let us make man[a] in our image, after our likeness. And let them have dominion over the fish of the sea and over the birds of the heavens and over the livestock and over all the earth and over every creeping thing that creeps on the earth."
>
> [27] So God created man in his own image,
>   in the image of God he created him;
>   male and female he created them.
>
> [28] And God blessed them. And God said to them, "Be fruitful and multiply and fill the earth and subdue it and have dominion over the fish of the sea and over the birds of the heavens and over every living thing that moves on the earth." [29] And God said, "Behold, I have given you every plant yielding seed that is on the face of all the earth, and every tree with seed in its fruit. You shall have them for food. [30] And to every beast of the earth and to every bird of the heavens and to everything that creeps on the earth, everything that has the breath of life, I have given every green plant for food." And it was so. [31] And God saw everything that he had made, and behold, it was very good. And there was evening and there was morning, the sixth day.

____

____

____

____

____

Everything He made, created, including us, was very good. The word good means exceptionally spectacular. He made all things in His creation to be exceptional—including us. He further states: Let us make man and woman in our image so we reflect Him. We have His characteristics. And—let's hand to them authority over the Earth, the stuff of the Earth, the physical things of the Earth. So, over the plants, the animals, the resources—Adam and Eve were going to become co-creators because, remember, they were in perfect communion with God. God didn't say, "I'm giving it to you. I'll see you later." He said: You're going to be a co-creator, a co-author of dominion with me, and I'm handing this over to you. And you rule Earth, not absent of Me, but in concert with Me.

> **Read Genesis 2:15:**
>
> 15 The LORD God took the man and put him in the garden of Eden to work it and keep it.

____

____

____

____

____

So, He says: work the garden, tend to the garden. The word *work* means have rulership over the garden, occupy, get to work. "You're in charge of those resources that I've created, and you are to have Authority." Life is going to involve supernatural things because you'll have the ability to exercise the spiritual power—speaking to the material, because that's how God did it. And that authority still exists. When God created the world by speaking it into existence, it was not just material or the natural, but spiritual, since it was subject to the authority of the spiritual. But when Adam and Eve exercised their free will (also in the image of God) and disobeyed God, they caused a colossal problem for the world—they gave authority away to Satan, the enemy.

Review and respond to the following three sets of verses. Though God established His original exceptional life for His children in a perfect place that was intended to be extended to all the Earth, what happened that this was interrupted and lost? Because of this, who then has the authority? As now we understand why receiving and exercising authority is a part of our current life, why is this so significant? Who gave the authority to the enemy?

Read Genesis 3:7; 22–24:

7 Then the eyes of both were opened, and they knew that they were naked. And they sewed fig leaves together and made themselves loincloths.

22 Then the Lord God said, "Behold, the man has become like one of us in knowing good and evil. Now, lest he reach out his hand and take also of the tree of life and eat and live forever—" 23 therefore the Lord God sent him out from the garden of Eden to work the ground from which he was taken. 24 He drove out the man, and at the east of the garden of Eden he placed the cherubim and a flaming sword that turned every way to guard the way to the tree of life.

____

____

____

____

____

What happened? God said to Adam and Eve: If you eat at that tree, you will surely do what? Die. And they did—they ate of the tree and died. They violated their instruction, which was meant to keep them fully experiencing this authority. "Stay with Me in fellowship, and in your created perfection (perfect capability with spirit, body, and soul in a perfect world), you will be co-creators with Me, exercising the authority I gave you. Having already fallen as a heavenly host through the exercise of his free will, the enemy appealed to Adam and Eve with the same self-will desire that caused him to fall—to become like God and take over ultimate authority. Interestingly enough, they already had it—in their proper role—created in the image of God to whom God had given authority as co-creators in concert with following His will through their being faithful to His truth and instruction.

Satan had great authority in heaven, but it wasn't enough. He wanted it all, but because he was a created being, and not God, he had no ability to gain it. God could not give it to him since he was seeking it against the authority and power of God, and thus Satan was cast out of heaven. God turned to the other angels and gave them the opportunity to choose who they would follow (again free will). One-third of the angels followed Satan and are now demons; and two-thirds followed God and are now angelic beings, living in the splendor and majesty of God.

Satan appeals to Adam and Eve, who already have the authority over the Earth, to want it all as well. *Did God really say that? Surely you will not die. Don't you want to be like God?* They were already like God, made in His image, so Satan was appealing to their self-will—to choose their own way—and at that moment, they did not check in with the Father to process and missed the essence of the relationship of privilege and truth. Just as spoken to them by God, they died, and their authority was lost. What happened to it? They gave it to Satan. They handed it over to Satan, because in essence they chose to follow and obey him. They then moved from the perfection of body, soul, and spirit in perfect communion with God in a perfect world to "sin nature" and the world was handed over to the enemy of kill, steal, and destroy; the authority that now controls the Earth is perverted. How? Instead of the world being in perfect harmony between spiritual and natural under God's goodness, beauty, and abundance, it is now under the enemy's control, whose nature is destruction and self-centeredness. All the offspring of Adam and Eve, including us, lost the spiritual life and its authority, and are now primarily living in the natural in difficulty, in trouble, under dominion of the enemy.

Read Luke 4:5–8:

[5] And the devil took him up and showed him all the kingdoms of the world in a moment of time, [6] and said to him, "To you I will give all this authority and their glory, for it has been delivered to me, and I give it to whom I will. [7] If you, then, will worship me, it will all be yours." [8] And Jesus answered him, "It is written,

"'You shall worship the Lord your God,
and him only shall you serve.'"

____

____

____

____

Was this a real temptation for Christ? Yes. If it wasn't real, Christ would have said, *What a fool. You don't have this to give to me. This is a hollow invitation.* Rather, He said, *Yes, I know that you, Satan, have authority over the kingdoms of the world.* Who gave it to him? Adam and Eve—and this will play out as to why authority is so critical for us. Satan appeals to Christ to take a shortcut and get back what Satan knows Christ has come to gain back—authority. Satan says, *All you have to do is worship me and together we'll have power over the Earth—you won't have to go to the cross.* But Jesus said what? *No. I've come to do the will of the Father, and the will of the Father is for Me to go a different way to get this authority back. I do admit you have the authority and it is real, but I'm not taking a shortcut with you.*

Read 1 John 5:18–20:

[18] We know that everyone who has been born of God does not keep on sinning, but he who was born of God protects him, and the evil one does not touch him.

[19] We know that we are from God, and the whole world lies in the power of the evil one.

[20] And we know that the Son of God has come and has given us understanding, so that we may know him who is true; and we are in him who is true, in his Son Jesus Christ. He is the true God and eternal life.

____

____

____

____

____

Sixty years after the resurrection, John says, "We know that the whole world lies under the authority, dominion, control of the evil one." So, does he still have this authority that is characterized by kill, steal, and destroy? Yes. Over what? The physical world, the natural. It's still under entropy. When Christ came and died on the cross and was resurrected, did He cure that issue? No. Rather He regained the supreme authority in His Kingdom to overrule the natural, and in that Kingdom, He is inviting His creation to:

1. Believe the truth of what He did to rectify the problem of the sin nature that separates us from God;

2. Walk with Him in His Kingdom by surrendering our will to the King of the Kingdom where the King (the Father) will have us receiving His authority and then take back the natural authority from whom we gave it to—Satan.

Can we do this on our own? No, we have no ability to take back the authority of Satan who has control over the natural. Rather, we must again rejoin God in the spiritual, and with His superior spiritual authority take back the authority of the natural. This explains much: In order for Christ to take the authority back, what did He have to become? A man. He had to become part of the creation to usher us into the place of taking back the authority. This is very profound. Is God more powerful than Satan? Yes. Did God create the world? Yes. Why didn't He just get rid of Satan, get rid of the world and its destructive nature, and start over? That would have been a lot easier, but there is free will involved—Satan's and mankind. How did He set it up in the first place? He created the world which was exceptionally good; and men and women in what? His image—to be the physical representation of the invisible God. And He gave authority to His creation made in His image over the exceptionally good creation of the world. So, according to His nature, He cannot then just destroy it all—it would have included His precious creation made in His image.

Rather, the Father sent His only son to become like man (subordinated His might and power to be that of a human) that then set up the opportunity for Him to take on the required penalty of death to bring life and restore the authority to mankind. Mankind, who receive the remedy, reborn with the life of the Spirit and overcome the death that excluded this life. The spirit again re-enters those who receive and then follow God in His Kingdom to receive the authority and then take back the authority from the enemy and the world. God's spiritual authority can again operate in this world and regain the intended supernatural life available to us.

LESSON 1:
WHAT IS THE AUTHORITY AND SUPERNATURAL WORK OF GOD?

What was the work that Jesus finished? Why was it necessary? How then are we to join Him in this work? Why?

> **Read John 17:1–5:**
>
> The High Priestly Prayer
>
> **17** When Jesus had spoken these words, he lifted up his eyes to heaven, and said, "Father, the hour has come; glorify your Son that the Son may glorify you, ² since you have given him authority over all flesh, to give eternal life to all whom you have given him. ³ And this is eternal life, that they know you, the only true God, and Jesus Christ whom you have sent. ⁴ I glorified you on earth, having accomplished the work that you gave me to do. ⁵ And now, Father, glorify me in your own presence with the glory that I had with you before the world existed.

____

____

____

____

____

Jesus finished the Father's work—the word finish means: completed to its end. He completed to its end the work of God. And now He's been given the authority to continue this work through His followers. What was the work? *I'm going to go to the cross and die, but then be resurrected. And in order for Me to go to My death, I have to go to Gethsemane.* And what happens there? Jesus battles His self-will. This is profound. Paul describes this in Romans 5:1–10; he says, by one man and woman, sin entered the world through what? Exercising their self-will in disobedience to the will of God. So, sin entered, mankind changed from perfection to a sinful, self-centered nature, handed over the authority of the world to Satan. The world is now a place of trouble—kill, steal, and destroy—a real problem caused by the one in the flesh. However, the victory was regained through Christ's what? His conquering the self-will. And that's why in Gethsemane, it had to be the battle of His will as a man. In John 10 it says that the Father is not going to help Him with this. This is going to be His battle. So, the real victory, interestingly enough, was where? In Gethsemane. He had to overcome the problem by conquering His will. Why did He go back in the garden a second time? He knew he wasn't there yet, because it was not settled in His heart—*My head says yes, but I haven't conquered the self, and I can't carry this out.* It is the same thing when He goes in a third time. It took Him three times in and out of the garden to conquer it—to finish the work of overcoming the self-will that created the spiritual problem of all mankind. *Not My will be done but Yours, Father.*

From the following three sets of verses, describe the elements of God's authority that will make an impact on how we are to live in this world controlled by the enemy. Why are these so significant to us?

Read Genesis 3:14–15:

14 The LORD God said to the serpent,
"Because you have done this,
    cursed are you above all livestock
    and above all beasts of the field;
on your belly you shall go,
    and dust you shall eat
    all the days of your life.
15 I will put enmity between you and the woman,
    and between your offspring[a] and her offspring;
he shall bruise your head,
    and you shall bruise his heel."

____

____

____

____

____

Christ crushes Satan's head—destroys his power and receives authority over the world and difficulties of life. Christ was bruised as He went to His death. But it doesn't end because He goes to what? The resurrection. I raise Him again into life. But you, Satan, are going to have your head crushed. And when did that all occur? At the Garden of Gethsemane—and then it was finished at the cross because He had to finish it with His death. Because Adam and Eve exercised their free will against the will of the Father, Christ had to regain it back by the exercise of His surrender—His will to the will of the Father. That's the issue of the flesh versus the spirit. Which means you have to conquer your will and go through your own Gethsemane. Of course, we've got to do it all the time to live the life of the spirit. So, He conquered it. And as He said at the cross, when He finished it with His death, certain things happened.

Read Colossians 2:11–15:

[11] In him also you were circumcised with a circumcision made without hands, by putting off the body of the flesh, by the circumcision of Christ, [12] having been buried with him in baptism, in which you were also raised with him through faith in the powerful working of God, who raised him from the dead. [13] And you, who were dead in your trespasses and the uncircumcision of your flesh, God made alive together with him, having forgiven us all our trespasses, [14] by canceling the record of debt that stood against us with its legal demands. This he set aside, nailing it to the cross. [15] He disarmed the rulers and authorities[a] and put them to open shame, by triumphing over them in him.[b]

____

____

____

____

____

We've got to understand the power of what He's done. Through His death, we've joined Him in that death. He's raised us up into the spiritual realm again. We are born again, and we're in the spiritual realm. Of course, we understand that we have to continue to choose this. Are we going to be in that realm with its authority or in the kingdom of the enemy where the enemy has power over us? He says He fulfilled the work:

1. He forgave all the sins of the world.

2. He took away the requirement or the obligation that is written against us. Because His nature being Holy, our requirement to have a relationship with Him is what? Perfection. Why did we lose the ability to do that? Because of the spiritual dying when we went to the flesh—sin nature, self-centeredness

by nature—so we could never be perfect by trying to be perfect—it was not possible. So, He just removed that requirement. The requirement now is just to believe what He gives us by grace.

3. He disarmed principalities and powers, so they now have no power over us when we live in His Kingdom. When you have a missile that needs to be disarmed, you simply take the trigger mechanism away. It can't fire. It's there, but it can't fire. The principalities and powers are there, and in the world, they have power over us, but in the Kingdom are disarmed—cannot work.

4. He gained triumph or victory over Satan, so he's now fully defeated—victory is complete, and there will no longer be a battle.

Read Matthew 28:1–8; 18–20:

The Resurrection

28 Now after the Sabbath, toward the dawn of the first day of the week, Mary Magdalene and the other Mary went to see the tomb. [2] And behold, there was a great earthquake, for an angel of the Lord descended from heaven and came and rolled back the stone and sat on it. [3] His appearance was like lightning, and his clothing white as snow. [4] And for fear of him the guards trembled and became like dead men. [5] But the angel said to the women, "Do not be afraid, for I know that you seek Jesus who was crucified. [6] He is not here, for he has risen, as he said. Come, see the place where he[a] lay. [7] Then go quickly and tell his disciples that he has risen from the dead, and behold, he is going before you to Galilee; there you will see him. See, I have told you." [8] So they departed quickly from the tomb with fear and great joy and ran to tell his disciples.

[18] And Jesus came and said to them, "All authority in heaven and on earth has been given to me. [19] Go therefore and make disciples of all nations, baptizing them in[a] the name of the Father and of the Son and of the Holy Spirit, [20] teaching them to observe all that I have commanded you. And behold, I am with you always, to the end of the age."

Let's put all this together. Man (humans) handed authority over to Satan. Satan says, *I have it*. The world under his authority is a very difficult place because the nature of the enemy is what? To kill, steal, and destroy, and it's relentless. It doesn't quit. And it's worldwide—everywhere, and all the people born into it are self-centered people with a desire to take advantage of that to manipulate how they can gain from this wicked world. So, there are a lot of problems in the world. John wrote 60 years later that the world is still under Satan's control. But wait a second. Christ was just resurrected, and He said all the authority and powers have been given to us. How do we reconcile those two things?

Jesus kept telling His disciples and numerous other people that the Kingdom of God is here—*I'm bringing My Kingdom, which is eternal. It's a spiritual Kingdom. I haven't come at this moment* (which, by the way, was a great disappointment to the disciples) *to take over politically and rule the world*. That's what their expectation was. Even after the resurrection, they ask Jesus in Acts 1:5: Is this the time that we're taking over? He says: *You still don't understand, do you? My Kingdom is spiritual and all authority has been given to Me, and I'm the ruler of this now*. This authority does not supplant the authority of the world under the control of the enemy, but rather this authority is superior to the world. Why? Because that's how the world was created. God spoke it into existence because the world is subordinate to the Spiritual Power of God where He can speak things into existence and into change. So, Satan still retains authority on Earth and can only be trumped in the spiritual realm. We can be trapped in the kingdom of the world where the enemy does have authority and power over the natural—but can be victorious over any power of the enemy when we live in God's Kingdom with all the superior authority, which completely trumps the authority of the enemy in the world.

Now, let's take that farther. Why doesn't the enemy have any authority in the Kingdom? Because God has triumphed over him and disarmed him. He has zero power in the Kingdom of God. So, it's not a battle of equals as Satan is not God, but a created being. He has lots of power, but no power relative to Christ. That's why Christ says all authority has been given to Him, including over the creation—but this only occurs when the Kingdom is operating. Things are getting very interesting.

Who is bringing the Kingdom? We are. In other words, we have to take it back. How? When we are living in the Kingdom of God, His authority extends to us and we're going to take it back—because living in the Kingdom means we are not living in the natural under the control of the enemy—rather in the spiritual, restoring the power of the Kingdom back to its rightful place, reclaiming what's been lost. How? Day by day, step by step, place by place, which is why it's not universal. It's not even universal as a church, because it's possible that a lot of people in that church or the leadership in that church are not walking in the

Kingdom, making the Kingdom smaller and smaller and smaller. But what does God want to do? Make it bigger and bigger and bigger.

How does that work? Consider yourself, your spouse, your kids, your small group. There's tremendous power available to us. If it's just you, that's OK, you can reclaim things back primarily through your life and your life circumstances. Remember, it is not universal nor everlasting. Why? Because Satan still has authority over the world, and we can step out of the Kingdom back into the world—from the authority of God to the authority of Satan. How? Choosing not to listen or choosing not to abide. Five minutes ago, I could have been walking in the Kingdom and enjoying the power of the Kingdom—and then I step into self, walk out of the Kingdom, and lose my access to power and thus encounter the trouble of the world in a big way.

We have the perfect example in Matthew 16:13–20 where Jesus asks the disciples, *Who do you guys say I am? John the Baptist? Elijah? Jeremiah? Who do you say I am?* Peter says, *Jesus the Christ, the Messiah.* Jesus responds, *This has been granted to you by My Father in heaven. You have great revelation and thus have received this revelation in the Spirit. Upon this profession, upon your understanding, upon your ability to hear God and walk into His Kingdom life, I will build My church. You will have the power (authority) to bind and loose. You are a most spiritual man in the Kingdom of God.* Ten minutes later, Christ said to Peter, *Get behind me, Satan.* Why? He stepped out of the Kingdom. We don't have the things He's got in mind. We have the things of what? By default, you've gone back to the kingdom of the enemy. It's moment by moment, it's day by day, and you can easily lose that power as you pursue the things you think are good ideas instead of surrendering to the King of the Kingdom. When you step outside the Kingdom, who's got more power than you? The enemy has way more power than you, and he has a lot of helpers. When you are in the world and not the Kingdom, you have no ability to counteract it. But when you step in the Kingdom, guess what? He can't touch you. This doesn't mean you don't have trouble because you're in the world. You live in both places—and this duality coexists. God transfers us into His Kingdom with authority and asks us to stay in His Kingdom to live out all the possibilities of this authority in a difficult world.

Let's look at where those who are not of Christ stand. John 3:16 says you stand condemned already, but God—who so loved the world, that He sent us His only begotten Son that whoever shall believe in Him shall not perish. But, having not believed you stand what? Condemned and under the authority and power of a troubled world, controlled by Satan—which means you will experience all the negative consequences of that which is kill, steal, and destroy. A quick look at the headlines of a newspaper or a news channel on TV or new website would reveal numerous examples of kill, steal, and destroy. Horrible stuff happens on a daily basis around the world. It is everywhere. So, if you live in France, are you exempt from that? No. Every place is experiencing the kill, steal, and destroy of the enemy—it's the nature of the world and because of how God set it up. He doesn't bypass us as we ask, *Why don't You just eliminate all evil? He said, No, you've got to take it back, but it requires you to live in the Kingdom.*

Though we are called to live in His Kingdom and exercise authority, what problem do we have as having fallen and who live with a sin nature? Why is this such an issue then for us living out the life of God's authority to restoration?

Read Romans 6:15–16; 7:14–23:

Slaves to Righteousness

15 What then? Are we to sin because we are not under law but under grace? By no means! 16 Do you not know that if you present yourselves to anyone as obedient slaves,[a] you are slaves of the one whom you obey, either of sin, which leads to death, or of obedience, which leads to righteousness?

14 For we know that the law is spiritual, but I am of the flesh, sold under sin. 15 For I do not understand my own actions. For I do not do what I want, but I do the very thing I hate. 16 Now if I do what I do not want, I agree with the law, that it is good. 17 So now it is no longer I who do it, but sin that dwells within me. 18 For I know that nothing good dwells in me, that is, in my flesh. For I have the desire to do what is right, but not the ability to carry it out. 19 For I do not do the good I want, but the evil I do not want is what I keep on doing. 20 Now if I do what I do not want, it is no longer I who do it, but sin that dwells within me.

21 So I find it to be a law that when I want to do right, evil lies close at hand. 22 For I delight in the law of God, in my inner being, 23 but I see in my members another law waging war against the law of my mind and making me captive to the law of sin that dwells in my members.

Paul's talking as a believer, and he says, *As much as I would like to, if I try to do this on my own flesh—trying to do the things I'm supposed to do and stop doing things I'm not supposed to do, I can't.* We can't do it. As believers, we are still under a law of the flesh that's operational. We can't bypass it. We can have a heart to bypass it, but we can't bypass it. Why? That's the nature of the world and the sin nature of all humans. As believers, absent of living in the Kingdom, we default back to the world of Satan, the kingdom of Satan, and living under the authority of Satan. We know non-believers live there, but as believers, we can live there, too. Because, he said, *If I try to operate in the flesh myself with the greatest of intentions, I still fall under the authority of the enemy.*

So, it's a matter of choice. It's binary. Who do you present yourself to? Paul told us there's a default to that. Either you live in the Kingdom by surrendering your will to the King or you, by default, live in the kingdom of the enemy—because you became a slave to self and therefore Satan. That's why Jesus can say to Peter, *Get behind me, Satan. You just exercised self, and you went away from the Kingdom into the world—you automatically became under the power and control of the enemy.* By what? By your choice. So, we, as believers, still have an interesting choice. Are we going to live in the Kingdom, or are we going to live in the flesh, in the self, in the world? And if we do, we are under the control of whom? The enemy. We likely do not just say we are going to follow the enemy today—it's about our surrender as we naturally follow self and thus operate in the flesh and under the world control of the enemy. We've learned to reinforce that for each other, as well, because Satan has tricked us. He said, *Well, God's in control. God's doing this to you. You're suffering because of God.* If that were true, what would you come to believe about God? He's not a good God. And Satan says, *Yeah, gotcha. Exactly.* When we buy that lie, we partner with Satan. As a believer, you're under the control, the authority of Satan. What is going to happen to you? Not good things. Kill, steal, and destroy. You're going to get attacked, bombarded, overwhelmed. You question how God could allow that? He said, *I didn't. You chose it. And I don't intervene in the authority of the world when my children are not with me in the Kingdom. Guess what? You gave it away. You've got to take it back. How do you take it back? Come back to the Kingdom.* And that's why evil, wicked stuff happens. And God says, *I'm not returning Garden of Eden. You gave that up. So, the world now is under the power and the control of the enemy. And that's why you're living out there. He's saying: Now, if I were you, I'd choose life instead of death; blessing instead of curses. And I invite you to this covenant and all the beautiful things of the covenant. But guess what? You have authority in the Kingdom—out in the world you have none.* Instead of questioning how God, who is supposed to love you, is letting that happen; we are to know the characteristics of the world and thus always desire to return to the life, beauty, and authority of God's Kingdom.

As we come to the conclusion of this first lesson, we've established that we were made in the image of Him to be the physical representation of the invisible God. He said, *Here, I'm giving you authority over the Earth in concert with Me.* It was always in that spiritual perfection. But we need to understand we are in the world and are subject to the authority and power of the enemy who has control over the world. We are not exempt from that, but we do have power and authority by surrendering to the King and living in the Kingdom. Our power comes from the Kingdom of God, which we will learn in the next lessons.

LESSON 2:
HOW DO WE EXPERIENCE GOD'S AUTHORITY, ESPECIALLY WHEN NEEDING TO HAVE DIFFICULT CIRCUMSTANCES RESTORED?

As we continue in this wonderful course: *Receiving and Exercising the Authority of God,* it's unique in that it puts things together and helps us understand our place in life and the opportunity we have with authority in our lives. Remember, God says He created the world by His authority—what He spoke, so His spiritual power is always superior to the material, to the natural. He then created Adam and Eve in His image to be co-creators and transferred that authority to them over the Earth. They were superior over the Earth. They were to continue to do supernatural things, miraculous things—develop, be fruitful and multiply, and take the perfection of the Garden of Eden, along with their perfection, and their intimate relationship with God into forever. We know that His image included free will and is part of His very nature. Satan had already exercised his free will by wanting to take the authority of God and was booted out of heaven along with the demons that followed him. Satan then goes to Adam and Eve and says: *Surely, you won't die like God has said.* And again, because they had perfect communion, they didn't go back to God and process that further.

Instead, they exercised their free will. And then what happened? Sin nature, the life of the flesh. They lost the spiritual authority, a spiritual power connected with God, and handed over the authority to Satan, who now is kill, steal, and destroy. Now we live in a difficult world, a wicked world, an evil world, a tough world, that's been this way since Adam and Eve gave it to Satan. Jesus acknowledged that Satan has authority over this world but said, *I'm not coming to get it that way* when Satan tried to tempt Him. And then, 60 years after the resurrection, John wrote, *All the world is still under the authority of God.* We find ourselves in this interesting place where Christ died for us, came back as a man, conquered self, and He now has authority. So how do these two, seemingly contradictory, statements line up? All authority has been given to Christ, and Satan has authority over the world. Well, it's a matter of where these truths are operationally—in two places. Christ's authority is operating in the Kingdom of God, which is a spiritual place. It's superior to the natural authority, which is under the control of Satan in the kingdom of the world. The world is still kill, steal, and destroy, and everybody born is born into that world. We, as believers, have the choice to make whether we surrender to live in the Kingdom or, by default, go back to the world of the enemy where we're going to be under the consequences of that wicked world.

Satan's authority in this natural world is superior to ours. We live in the natural by default, and then we have a choice to be able to live in both places. When we go to the Kingdom of God, we have now the authority of God that is far superior to the enemy's world. It's really an interesting thing that explains a lot. A lot of believers say, *How did God allow this awful or difficult circumstance to happen? I thought He was in control.* He says: *Well, it's structural. It's because you gave authority over to this wicked enemy who now has it, and the nature of the world is now entropy—kill, steal, and destroy.* That's how the world functions. You cannot reverse this per se (wish that God would just eliminate all evil and adversity), which we'll learn today. And He's not causing the problem. Rather, given the problem, He enjoys the opportunity to recover and restore the problem.

We know that the nature of Satan's authority is to steal, kill, and destroy. Does that nature change? No. Is it relentless? Yes. It's the nature of the enemy, and by definition, the nature of the world is also kill, steal, and destroy. So, that explains things, doesn't it? Wars, murders, theft, conflict, oppression, difficulty, annoyance, frustration, etc. The enemy, who is in opposition to the life and work of God, is going to take your stuff, going to overcome you, doesn't care about you, will come in battle against you, will be in conflict with you, will be fighting you. And it goes all the way from a national/global level down to individuals, as couples, as families, churches, which brings up a question many have: How can people in the Christian church be fighting with each other? I thought God was love. Well, He is. But guess what? They're not walking with Him. They're walking in the natural world (not in the Kingdom of God) and are subject to the nature of the world—kill, steal, and destroy. This means awful things happen all the time: disease, weather issues, accidents, things fall apart, problems at work, problems with family. Difficult things happen. Why? Because we live in a difficult place; because the nature of Satan who has control over it is to kill, steal, and destroy.

Based on our perspective of the way the world is structured, it is getting worse and going to keep getting worse. While there are people who believe the world is getting better and better and better, if you sit down and talk to them, you come to realize that they just have a philosophy that it is going to get better. They likely believe that politics is what can stimulate that, but God has reminded us to simply look at the history of the world. Have you ever seen a political agenda make anything truly better—from any party? Some may idealize certain eras or epochs, but if we were to truly experience life then, we would understand that the world is and has always been controlled and under the domain of the enemy. The good news is that God's Kingdom is superior, and we can live in this superior place that restores and overcomes the difficult world.

From what has God promised to restore us to His exceptional life? Why do we have these issues (world under the control of enemy and our sin nature)? How will He be able to restore us since we have a problem of the sin nature and the world is so difficult? Why is this important for us to live this out?

Read Isaiah 61:1–4:

The Year of the LORD'S Favor
61 The Spirit of the LORD GOD is upon me,
  because the LORD has anointed me
to bring good news to the poor;[a]
  he has sent me to bind up the brokenhearted,
to proclaim liberty to the captives,
  and the opening of the prison to those who are bound;[b]
2 to proclaim the year of the LORD'S favor,
  and the day of vengeance of our God;
  to comfort all who mourn;
3 to grant to those who mourn in Zion—
  to give them a beautiful headdress instead of ashes,
the oil of gladness instead of mourning,
  the garment of praise instead of a faint spirit;
that they may be called oaks of righteousness,
  the planting of the LORD, that he may be glorified.[c]
4 They shall build up the ancient ruins;
  they shall raise up the former devastations;
they shall repair the ruined cities,
  the devastations of many generations.

____

____

____

____

____

He says He's coming to restore this difficult place and describes our broken heartedness. We thought life was going to be better, but we just can't get there. Things are broken, captive. We are bound up. We have tried to get out of these patterns and our nature won't let us. We are trying to stop it but can't. We get angry, fearful, anxious. We go to addiction, to conflict, to arguing and fighting. We try to stop it but can't. There's mourning and sadness. What are we sad for? Things we've lost. We mourn because we had it and experienced it, but now have lost it. We used to have financial freedom and we're back in bondage now. We were running a company that was doing really well, but now we're really struggling, and we're mourning that. Ashes, our life can become ashes, which are worthless. We begin to lose hope. Why bother? We figure, *This is it*, and we drift to a level of mediocrity. We've accepted that life is just going to be a struggle. Heaviness. The spirit of heaviness is apparent as we are losing hope and don't see a way out or a way to victory. It's just going to be slugging in the mud when it feels like everything is wasted, ruined, deserted. It doesn't work. We look at our life and think, *It's wasted, ruined, filled with issues*. What do all those circumstances describe? Kill, steal, and destroy. Is that God's purpose? No. What does Satan say? *My world is a hard place, and it's always going to be a hard place*. Even now, two thousand years after Christ, most believers would look at their life and say they, too, were experiencing this hardship, but they've got a ticket to heaven so they just put up with it. You get to go to heaven, and that's going to be great, but your life down here is going to be hard. Why? Because that's the nature of the world. We're not immune from that because that's the way the world now operates.

What are the important elements of God's dominion? Why are these to be experienced by us then? Why?

> **Read 1 Chronicles 29:11–15:**
>
> [11] Yours, O LORD, is the greatness and the power and the glory and the victory and the majesty, for all that is in the heavens and in the earth is yours. Yours is the kingdom, O LORD, and you are exalted as head above all. [12] Both riches and honor come from you, and you rule over all. In your hand are power and might, and in your hand it is to make great and to give strength to all. [13] And now we thank you, our God, and praise your glorious name.
>
> [14] "But who am I, and what is my people, that we should be able thus to offer willingly? For all things come from you, and of your own have we given you. [15] For we are strangers before you and sojourners, as all our fathers were. Our days on the earth are like a shadow, and there is no abiding.[a]

____

____

____

____

____

He describes His Kingdom as authority: majesty, greatness, power, honor, riches—making things great. I'm going to strengthen you. Compare those things next to each other: the enemy's kill, steal, and destroy versus God Kingdom—majesty, power, might, strength, resolution of the enemy's world. You're going to enjoy what He gives you because there's no destruction there. There's no negative. We need to understand there are two kingdoms so that we don't attribute Satan's kingdom to God. God's nature is to bring it to greatness, not to kill, steal, and destroy. He's not saying that instead of living in His Kingdom, we are relegated to the life of difficulty in a difficult world. John 10:10 says: _I've come to give you life and give it to you super abundantly_. These are the same words that we read under God's authority in Genesis 1:31 when He said, _Everything I've made is exceptionally good_. Very, very good, abundantly good. Jesus said that's what He's come to do—restore that back from the difficulty of the world to those who are living in His Kingdom. Why? Because the enemy is destroying what God always planned to give. He's come to give you that restoration back—in our lives and in our hearts. _My power, My desire is for you to live with Me where I will restore that_. In other words, you won't be subject to a life that has to accept kill, steal, and destroy. You're living there, and you're going to be impacted by that (not exempted from this world). But He'll restore it to you.

Given we live in a difficult place with a sin nature, what are God's promises to restore us from these issues? Why is this so important and encouraging to us?

Re-read Isaiah 61:1–4:

The Year of the LORD'S Favor

61 The Spirit of the Lord God is upon me,
   because the Lord has anointed me
to bring good news to the poor;[a]
   he has sent me to bind up the brokenhearted,
to proclaim liberty to the captives,
   and the opening of the prison to those who are bound;[b]
² to proclaim the year of the LORD'S favor,
   and the day of vengeance of our God;
   to comfort all who mourn;
³ to grant to those who mourn in Zion—
   to give them a beautiful headdress instead of ashes,
the oil of gladness instead of mourning,
   the garment of praise instead of a faint spirit;
that they may be called oaks of righteousness,
   the planting of the LORD, that he may be glorified.[c]
⁴ They shall build up the ancient ruins;
   they shall raise up the former devastations;
they shall repair the ruined cities,
   the devastations of many generations.

____

____

____

____

____

We understand the kill, steal, and destroy part. What does Christ bring? Healing, binding up the broken heartedness. Liberty, opening up the prison. He's going to give us freedom so that we no longer live in captivity. He's going to comfort us in our mourning. He's going to restore that. We will have hope and beauty. The things we've ruined, He's going to make beautiful. He's going to give us joy. He's going to have us praise instead of being burdened with heaviness and the weight of the things we've ruined. He's talking about real things, not just a spiritual dimension. He'll do what? He'll rebuild it. He'll restore it. Why? It's not a natural maneuvering that we're smarter than everybody else in the world and we're going to manipulate things better. He's going change it because He can speak to it. That's where His authority comes—in the Kingdom that is superior to the world. And the result? It's going to impact that world.

God clearly says it's not a matter of managing it better—He's not just going to cover it up. He's not just going to mask it. He's not just going to lessen its impact. No, He's going to replace it. He is going to restore it. He is going to give us the very best of life.

We know that the Kingdom of God (Romans 14:17) is righteousness, peace, and joy in the Holy Spirit. In the Kingdom, there's no kill, steal, and destroy. The Kingdom is shalom—extreme favor, Christ's righteousness. Christ reigning—justice is served. Joy. As you function in that Kingdom, in the Holy Spirit, the power is there to live out righteousness, peace, and joy. The Kingdom of God is always righteousness, peace, joy, restoration, and redeeming—not managing it.

From the following four sets of verses, what are the supernatural results of God's restoration of life's problems caused by the enemy? What should we then expect, and why is this so important to us?

Read Matthew 8:1–3:

Jesus Cleanses a Leper

8 When he came down from the mountain, great crowds followed him. [2] And behold, a leper[a] came to him and knelt before him, saying, "Lord, if you will, you can make me clean." [3] And Jesus[b] stretched out his hand and touched him, saying, "I will; be clean." And immediately his leprosy was cleansed.

____

____

____

____

____

Jesus was asked: If You would, could You heal me? And Jesus said, *What? Sure. How about if I do it right now*. He's got a physical problem. He's living in the world caused by what? Kill, steal, and destroy. He has leprosy, which at that point wasn't curable. People with leprosy were isolated, sent away because of its contagiousness. They couldn't touch anything, couldn't be with anybody, and were sent away. But he found his way to Jesus. Could You heal me? *Yes, by the power and authority of God*. He didn't say: Well, let Me get you some really good bandages or let Me give you some advice. This is how you could exist with leprosy, and I'll make it a little bit easier for you. He said, *My authority will heal it, because that's My heart*.

Read Matthew 8:5–13:

The Faith of a Centurion

5 When he had entered Capernaum, a centurion came forward to him, appealing to him, 6 "Lord, my servant is lying paralyzed at home, suffering terribly." 7 And he said to him, "I will come and heal him." 8 But the centurion replied, "Lord, I am not worthy to have you come under my roof, but only say the word, and my servant will be healed. 9 For I too am a man under authority, with soldiers under me. And I say to one, 'Go,' and he goes, and to another, 'Come,' and he comes, and to my servant,[a] 'Do this,' and he does it." 10 When Jesus heard this, he marveled and said to those who followed him, "Truly, I tell you, with no one in Israel[b] have I found such faith. 11 I tell you, many will come from east and west and recline at table with Abraham, Isaac, and Jacob in the kingdom of heaven, 12 while the sons of the kingdom will be thrown into the outer darkness. In that place there will be weeping and gnashing of teeth." 13 And to the centurion Jesus said, "Go; let it be done for you as you have believed." And the servant was healed at that very moment.

____

____

____

____

____

The centurion is a Roman soldier who is not really religious, but he's been observing Christ and has a servant who is sick. He goes to Jesus and says, *Could you come and heal him?* And Jesus said, *Yes.* The centurion then says, *Actually, I'm not worthy of you coming to my place, why don't you just speak it, and it'll be taken care of?* And Jesus's response is what? *Wow, even my disciples don't get this, but you got it.* And the centurion explained it. *I've been observing you and I noticed something. When you heal people, you say something, you speak to it, and your power is realized. He says, I'm a man under authority. When I say something, it happens. That's what it's all about, isn't it? Your spiritual power is superior to this material stuff, isn't it? Yeah. So, you know what? Why don't you just speak it? And that'll be the end of it?* Jesus said, *You got it. It is done.* His authority is superior to the material, to the natural. So, regarding the problems we have, God says, *Nothing is too difficult for Me.* Why? *My authority is superior to everything.* Let's see how that plays out.

Read Matthew 8:14–15:

Jesus Heals Many
14 And when Jesus entered Peter's house, he saw his mother-in-law lying sick with a fever. 15 He touched her hand, and the fever left her, and she rose and began to serve him.

____

____

____

____

____

When Jesus entered Peter's house, He saw his mother-in-law lying sick with a fever. He touched her hand, left her, and she rose and began to serve Him. Peter's mother-in-law was so sick, she couldn't function. So, what does Jesus do? He touches her, and she gets up and starts serving—it's over, done with just His touch. It wasn't a long prayer meeting. It wasn't, *Here are some pills to take*. It was simply, *I have the authority; you have a problem. I am going to heal you right now—* and she got up and went back to work.

Read Matthew 8:16–17:

16 That evening they brought to him many who were oppressed by demons, and he cast out the spirits with a word and healed all who were sick. 17 This was to fulfill what was spoken by the prophet Isaiah: "He took our illnesses and bore our diseases."

____

____

____

____

____

Because of His authority being demonstrated by His healing, everybody nearby came to Him for healing. How many did He heal? All of those who went to Him. He said this was to fulfill what was spoken by Isaiah in Chapter 5: He went to his death to forgive us our sins—and by His stripes, healing restoration. This is more than just physical things, it's full restoration. He has come to bring restoration, and He fulfilled that at the cross. So, because He received this full authority at the cross—over invisible and visible in all creation, He now can exercise it here in our life through His authority over all issues of life. No formula. There are no requirements. He did it by touch. He did it by speaking. He did it close-up. He did it at a distance. He did it by simply thinking about it. Wow.

From the following two sets of verses, what is important for us to understand about the availability and significance of supernatural work under God's authority that we are to experience? Why are these so important to how we live His life out?

Read Ephesians 1:16–21:

[16] I do not cease to give thanks for you, remembering you in my prayers, [17] that the God of our Lord Jesus Christ, the Father of glory, may give you the Spirit of wisdom and of revelation in the knowledge of him, [18] having the eyes of your hearts enlightened, that you may know what is the hope to which he has called you, what are the riches of his glorious inheritance in the saints, [19] and what is the immeasurable greatness of his power toward us who believe, according to the working of his great might [20] that he worked in Christ when he raised him from the dead and seated him at his right hand in the heavenly places, [21] far above all rule and authority and power and dominion, and above every name that is named, not only in this age but also in the one to come.

He said He's been resurrected into the place where all authority is superior to the principalities and powers to the world, the natural. And He said that resurrection power, which is the greatest power ever, is directed toward whom? Those of us who believe. He gives us a little hint. This resurrected power authority is going to manifest itself in our life if we what? Believe. Believe what? That as we walk with Him in the Kingdom, we will experience this power directed toward our life circumstances. It's not generic or broad or directed only toward others. He says that it's actually directed toward us along the path to experience His supernatural, resurrection power. Why? He has it. He loves us and wants us to experience what He has to give us—freely and wonderfully.

Read Hebrews 2:1–4:

Warning Against Neglecting Salvation
2 Therefore we must pay much closer attention to what we have heard, lest we drift away from it. [2] For since the message declared by angels proved to be reliable, and every transgression or disobedience received a just retribution, [3] how shall we escape if we neglect such a great salvation? It was declared at first by the Lord, and it was attested to us by those who heard, [4] while God also bore witness by signs and wonders and various miracles and by gifts of the Holy Spirit distributed according to his will.

He said the salvation described in Isaiah 61:1–4 and in John 10:10 (life, super abundantly) will be demonstrated by what? Signs and wonders, miracles, and gifts of the Holy Spirit, according to God's will. He said, *I will bring about verification that this authority is real*. How? Things will happen that can only be fulfilled supernaturally by Him speaking to it—Him bringing about His power. He can take that leper and completely cleanse him instantaneously. He can heal that servant instantaneously because He has that power, has that authority. Nothing is too difficult for Him. So, don't neglect so great an opportunity. He's going to bear witness with authority.

We are not just to ask that God takes care of things; and hope He does (though rarely believe He will). When people are asked: Do you think God can do miracles? Most people say yes, even though they say it is unlikely for them or they have not experienced this personally. There's even a whole group of people who say it doesn't exist anymore. But this is not true. The scriptures never said it's over. God is the same yesterday, today, and tomorrow. His nature is the same, which is to give us life and give it to us super abundantly. It's not to manage life a little better. It's not to restore it and replace it with His life, which is superior, we have to be involved here with the understanding that we (through Adam and Eve) gave away the authority; and now we have to take it back. Can we do it by ourselves? No, because when we walk out of the Kingdom, we have departed from the source of the authority to be exercised through us—the power of Christ.

From the following verses, why does God send us out to exercise His authority? What should we then expect, and why are we to be part of this work here on Earth?

Read Luke 9:1–2; 10:1; 10:17–20:

Jesus Sends Out the Twelve Apostles
9 And he called the twelve together and gave them power and authority over all demons and to cure diseases, 2 and he sent them out to proclaim the kingdom of God and to heal.

Jesus Sends Out the Seventy-Two
10 After this the Lord appointed seventy-two[a] others and sent them on ahead of him, two by two, into every town and place where he himself was about to go.

The Return of the Seventy-Two
17 The seventy-two returned with joy, saying, "Lord, even the demons are subject to us in your name!" 18 And he said to them, "I saw Satan fall like lightning from heaven. 19 Behold, I have given you authority to tread on serpents and scorpions, and over all the power of the enemy, and nothing shall hurt you. 20 Nevertheless, do not rejoice in this, that the spirits are subject to you, but rejoice that your names are written in heaven."

____

____

____

____

____

God says that He is sending us out, and He's giving us authority. He has it. He's giving it to us. We are the Kingdom (Christ in us); we're walking in the Kingdom wherever we go. We're bringing the Kingdom into this wicked world under the authority of Christ. Since we live in the world, we are in both places. But what are we bringing if we're walking in the Kingdom? We are bringing the superior authority of Christ. We understand that things are difficult, but we are not supposed to be resigned to accepting the difficulty.

Instead, we are to seek out how we can bring superior power and authority to these difficult circumstances. Why? We're living in the Kingdom, and this authority resides in the Kingdom. That's why He kept saying, *Tell them the Kingdom is here.* Then, as others start to experience that authority and see fantastic stuff, their question would be what? How can I experience that Kingdom? We respond by helping them understand that this authority is available to them as they learn to live in the Kingdom. God did not say, *You guys wait here. I'll go do a few things, and then I'll come back and let you know how it went.* What did he say? Go with forward with the power and authority that He's giving us. We are the ones to exercise this authority.

From the following four sets of verses: As we experience this authority, what are we called to do for others who do not yet understand or experience this authority? Why is this so important? What role are we to have in doing the supernatural works using His authority? Why?

Read Matthew 28:18–20:

18 And Jesus came and said to them, "All authority in heaven and on earth has been given to me. 19 Go therefore and make disciples of all nations, baptizing them in[a] the name of the Father and of the Son and of the Holy Spirit, 20 teaching them to observe all that I have commanded you. And behold, I am with you always, to the end of the age."

____

____

____

____

____

He says to teach others what we have observed. He said to all this disciples, *What have you been observing for three years? My power and My authority; and I gave it to you. Do you understand all that?* So, it is because of this authority that He didn't say to do a bunch of Bible studies and teach them about Him and tell them that they're just going to get saved. Instead, He tells them that it's emanating out of what? The authority that we have been given. Go and make disciples and teach others to enjoy and receive this authority. Share what we have experienced. That's what a disciple maker is.

LESSON 2:
HOW DO WE EXPERIENCE GOD'S AUTHORITY, ESPECIALLY WHEN NEEDING TO HAVE DIFFICULT CIRCUMSTANCES RESTORED?

Read John 17:13–14:

13 But now I am coming to you, and these things I speak in the world, that they may have my joy fulfilled in themselves. 14 I have given them your word, and the world has hated them because they are not of the world, just as I am not of the world.

____

____

____

____

____

Jesus is praying to the Father that we are to be walking with Him and experiencing His word. Our natural thought would be: *Can't You just remove us from this place so we don't have to experience this all this?* He says, *No. I'm not asking the Father to remove you from that place. Actually, what I'm doing is the opposite. I'm sending you into it.* We must think about the nature of God. Is He sending us there to get attacked, to suffer, to get beat down? No, He's sending us into that place with power and authority. His word is superior to the difficult things of the world. He's not asking the Father to take us out. He's sending us in there with gusto and without fear. Why? Because we have that power and authority. We are going to be victorious. Yes, this is a bad place. It's tough. Rather than accepting it and living with it, knowing we at least get to go to heaven, we are to understand that we have authority and can speak to these difficulties and see things happen and be restored. The key is that we must be of and in the Kingdom and are not to be of the world where supernatural things will not happen.

Read John 14:12:

[12] Truly, truly, I say to you, whoever believes in me will also do the works that I do; and greater works than these will he do, because I am going to the Father.

____

____

____

____

He says: *Who's going to do the works?* We are. We're going to do greater works than Him. He's not talking about magnitude here. Can you do any better than the resurrection? No. He's not saying we'll be doing more magnificent miracles. He's saying that we'll be doing literally a greater number of these for the simple reason that there are now more of us who are supposed to be performing these miracles.

When He was doing miracles in Nazareth, they kicked Him out because of their unbelief. What was His reaction? He was dumbfounded. He said He was there to do these fantastic miracles for them, and they were refusing to be persuaded that He had this ability and power to do this on their behalf. They told Him to go and not perform what was on His heart to perform. That's why He says to His children now that there are very few people experiencing the supernatural. He's dumbfounded. He sent us because we were supposed to do a greater number and that everybody would be experiencing it. He's sending us into the world with the authority of the Kingdom. Why aren't we exercising it? Of course, it's a very simple reason why not. We don't live in the Kingdom. We, in the flesh, think we can do better in managing our difficult lives. He says we need to get ready to do these wonderful miracles.

Read Acts 1:6–8:

The Ascension

6 So when they had come together, they asked him, "Lord, will you at this time restore the kingdom to Israel?" 7 He said to them, "It is not for you to know times or seasons that the Father has fixed by his own authority. 8 But you will receive power when the Holy Spirit has come upon you, and you will be my witnesses in Jerusalem and in all Judea and Samaria, and to the end of the earth."

____

____

____

____

____

He says, *You don't quite yet get it, but you will. My Kingdom is spiritual.* He tells His disciples that they are going into the world and will receive what? Power and authority through the gift of the Holy Spirit that's going to enter them and then they will start exercising that power. But they have got to wait a bit longer because they don't quite yet have it. Why? It's not natural, it's supernatural by Him working through them, with them doing the work. They are to go out as the physical representation of the invisible God, who is living in them with all the power and authority that is now theirs.

What happened? At Pentecost, the Spirit came on them; Peter stood up with that authority, and how many people came to know Him? Three thousand. What did the 3,000 people do? Met in small groups and home churches. And what was happening in those small groups and home churches? Miracles, the supernatural. They said they were in awe at the authority and power of God, which He does by (as mentioned in Hebrews 2:1–4) bearing witness with signs and wonders. An exercise in authority. And guess what? They experienced it. This happened. Every day, more and more people came because they saw miracles, and they saw the power. So, what was their natural curiosity and heart? They would like to experience that, too. To do that, they had to learn to abide—to get connected to the vine; to walk in the Spirit, to live in the Kingdom of God.

LESSON 2:
HOW DO WE EXPERIENCE GOD'S AUTHORITY, ESPECIALLY WHEN NEEDING TO HAVE DIFFICULT CIRCUMSTANCES RESTORED?

As we experience and exercise His authority, how does our free will play a big part in this process? Why then is this not automatic and so important for us to choose? Choose what?

Read Deuteronomy 30:11–20:

The Choice of Life and Death

11 "For this commandment that I command you today is not too hard for you, neither is it far off. 12 It is not in heaven, that you should say, 'Who will ascend to heaven for us and bring it to us, that we may hear it and do it?' 13 Neither is it beyond the sea, that you should say, 'Who will go over the sea for us and bring it to us, that we may hear it and do it?' 14 But the word is very near you. It is in your mouth and in your heart, so that you can do it.

15 "See, I have set before you today life and good, death and evil. 16 If you obey the commandments of the Lord your God[a] that I command you today, by loving the Lord your God, by walking in his ways, and by keeping his commandments and his statutes and his rules,[b] then you shall live and multiply, and the Lord your God will bless you in the land that you are entering to take possession of it. 17 But if your heart turns away, and you will not hear, but are drawn away to worship other gods and serve them, 18 I declare to you today, that you shall surely perish. You shall not live long in the land that you are going over the Jordan to enter and possess. 19 I call heaven and earth to witness against you today, that I have set before you life and death, blessing and curse. Therefore choose life, that you and your offspring may live, 20 loving the Lord your God, obeying his voice and holding fast to him, for he is your life and length of days, that you may dwell in the land that the Lord swore to your fathers, to Abraham, to Isaac, and to Jacob, to give them."

God says: *In this Covenant life, I'm going to bless you to make you a blessing. This isn't difficult. It's not complicated. I set before you life or death, blessing or cursing.* He says, *If I were you, I'd choose life.* The word *life* is the vigorous, exceptional life of God. How does that occur since we are living in a wicked place? How do we get that life in the Kingdom and access to this authority so we can experience supernatural? God asks, *Are you going to come with Me or are you going to go on your own? Come with Me.* The authority will be exercised and we will be able to exercise it if we choose to participate in this. Our default is to go back to the world, but He wants us to choose life and blessings—rather than death (separation from the power and source of power) and cursing—opposite of blessing and living with the consequences of a difficult world with difficult circumstances.

Review and respond to the following three verses in Romans 6. Since receiving and exercising authority requires us to live in His Kingdom, how do we enter and remain living in His Kingdom? What is the result of living in His Kingdom?

Read Romans 6:7:

7 For one who has died has been set free[a] from sin.

What tense is used in "We have been set free"? Past tense. It is already done. We have been set free. We receive Christ as our Lord and Savior, we're set free. Then He makes a statement as a progression in the following verse.

Read Romans 6:18:

18 and, having been set free from sin, have become slaves of righteousness.

____

____

____

____

____

We've been set free. Now we have a choice to make. Are we going to serve Him or not? If we want freedom and power, who do we have to surrender to? To Christ—we have to become slaves of Christ, bond servants. We have to follow Him in the Kingdom as opposed to ourselves, which is our default. We must not be a slave to self. If we are, we go back to prison because we chose not to walk with Him as His bondservants. We are not going to be set free and experience the beautiful life that God desires to give His servants.

Read Romans 6:22:

22 But now that you have been set free from sin and have become slaves of God, the fruit you get leads to sanctification and its end, eternal life.

____

____

____

____

____

In John 17:3, Christ defined eternal life. It is knowing Him, experiencing Him and the Father—the power of God. The result of being a bondservant, of living in the Kingdom, will be what? Fruit of holiness—righteousness, power, might, the beautiful authority of the Kingdom. We do not chase it or try to be holy and righteous—rather we receive it by being His slave and then experiencing the fruit promised.

In order to receive this authority, what are we to ask for from the Father? What does this mean, and why is this so critical to our ability to receive and exercise authority?

Read 1 Kings 3:5–9:

5 At Gibeon the Lord appeared to Solomon in a dream by night, and God said, "Ask what I shall give you." 6 And Solomon said, "You have shown great and steadfast love to your servant David my father, because he walked before you in faithfulness, in righteousness, and in uprightness of heart toward you. And you have kept for him this great and steadfast love and have given him a son to sit on his throne this day. 7 And now, O Lord my God, you have made your servant king in place of David my father, although I am but a little child. I do not know how to go out or come in. 8 And your servant is in the midst of your people whom you have chosen, a great people, too many to be numbered or counted for multitude. 9 Give your servant therefore an understanding mind to govern your people, that I may discern between good and evil, for who is able to govern this your great people?"

____

____

____

____

____

When asked what he wants from God, Solomon says he first wants to approach everything as if he's a little kid. How does the little kid approach everything? Hey, Dad, Mom, what do you have to say about this? I'll follow you because I don't know. And you do. Solomon says that no matter how sophisticated he gets, he's going to seek God in everything. And God says: My joy is having you walk with Me and letting Me give super abundant life to you.

Solomon then asks for a hearing heart so that he can live a life of good versus evil, discerning between good and evil. As we ask this for us, we are asking for the ability to hear what? God's voice: not what we can figure out on our own but let us hear His voice. His word is what? Authority. It's superior to the material. He's going to speak to this issue, this problem, this difficulty and let us hear what He says about this. We will receive it, believe it, and speak it—and then we will see it happen. It'll be the difference between good and evil. The word evil used here isn't dark, awful, black. It's the things that annoy, frustrate, irritate, and come against us. So, we are asking for wisdom—to hear what God says, for God to give us the ability (freely available) to hear His authority so we can exercise it in this natural situation. Give us the clarity to hear what He has to say—which is where all the fun of life is and the joy for Him as He brings us into His joy.

As we finish Lesson 2, we've come to understand a few things:

1. The nature of the enemy's authority is kill, steal, and destroy, and that describes the world. It shouldn't surprise us that there are all kinds of problems in the world. Problems with people, problems with friends, problems with relatives.

2. Christ has superior authority, and He received it through surrendering His will, going to His death and then living in the resurrection, where all the superior power is in this Kingdom. He said we are to live in both places. He's not taking us out of this awful place, but He's sending us into it with what? Authority. He's giving it to us to exercise. It's not going to be His bypassing us. We gave it away, and now we have to take it back.

3. We have to live in the Kingdom and then exercise that authority how? We have to live in the Kingdom by surrendering to Him as a bondservant; and then ask Him to speak—then speak what He speaks. We will then experience it and will be doing the work of this authority, and we'll see redemption, we'll see restoration, we'll see the supernatural. We'll see a fantastic life of fantastic joy that only God can do through us.

LESSON 3:
WHAT IS IT WE ARE TO EXPECT AS WE EXPERIENCE GOD'S AUTHORITY AND SUPERNATURAL WORKS IN OUR PERSONAL LIVES?

As we complete our course: *Receiving and Exercising the Authority of God*, we're going to answer the following question: What is our position with authority and how do we exercise this authority? We've learned that God has the authority. His original intention was to have us join Him because we were created in His image. He handed over to men and women the authority over the Earth, and we were to be co-creators with Him—experiencing supernatural things on Earth as the perfection of the Garden of Eden would have been promoted throughout the world with people who were walking with God.

When Adam and Eve exercised their free will and chose to disobey God, they died to their spiritual connectivity and the power of the Holy Spirit and thus, their access and use of God's authority. The authority was handed over to Satan, who reinforced that when he tried to tempt Christ. As John said in 1 John 5:18–20, all the world is under the authority, the control of the evil one, which explains the kill, steal, and destroy and all of the difficulty and trouble and awfulness of life. This includes all the self-centered people operating on Earth who have a desire to kill, steal, and destroy as well because they don't care. We live in a difficult place but because of what Christ did, going to the cross on His own volition and forgiving everybody, He gave us all the opportunity to receive life from Him.

We believers have another choice. Are we now going to deny self, take up the cross and follow Him, and start to exercise that authority? Or are we going to be in the carnal, the flesh where we're operating as practical atheists? We're part of the family, and we have an eternal place with Him in heaven, but we are not going to be experiencing that authority here on earth. God says: *Because you gave it away, you have to take it back.* He doesn't bypass us but instead says that His authority will be exercised through us. As we talked about in the last lesson, receiving it is a choice. He says: *I set before you, life or death, blessing or curse, and you have to choose to walk with Me.* We then went to Romans 6:7, 18, and 22 where we saw the progression: We have been set free, we're part of the family, but now we have another choice to make. He asks, *Are you going to become My*

> "We've learned that God has the authority. His original intention was to have us join Him because we were created in His image."

slave (bondservant)? Are you going to serve Me and walk with Me so that I can give you this life in this authority? Or absent of that, we default back to what? The flesh, the sin nature. We now have gone back to living as Adam and Eve did after the fall—which is essentially trying to figure out life on our own.

If we choose Him and become part of the family, we have decided to follow Him. The result of that is fruit—the life that He has planned through exercising the authority that He says now is available for us. But we have to ask for it, ask for the ability to hear His word, which is the source of the authority. Remember, He said that the world was created by Him speaking it—that's where the authority comes in, the spiritual is superior to the material—God speaking it. When asked, Solomon said, What I need is to hear Your voice so I can exercise that authority.

In the middle of adversity caused by self-centered people in a wicked world, how did God provide the Covenant life to Joseph through His authority? On what basis did God provide this to Joseph? What then did Joseph experience, and how was this part of God's bigger story? What can we learn from this for us?

> **Read Genesis 39:22–23:**
>
> 22 And the keeper of the prison put Joseph in charge of all the prisoners who were in the prison. Whatever was done there, he was the one who did it. 23 The keeper of the prison paid no attention to anything that was in Joseph's charge, because the Lord was with him. And whatever he did, the Lord made it succeed.

____

____

____

____

____

We know the story of Joseph—his brothers wanted to get rid of him because of his dream of the coat of many colors. They put him in a hole, and the Egyptians captured him. First, he gets favor with Pharaoh and comes into his house—being put in a place of leadership in a foreign place, which is an illustration of the Covenant. When God blesses us to make us a blessing, it doesn't matter where we are. Yes, things happen and we might end up in a different place, but He's going to give us favor, which he did.

What then happened? Pharaoh's wife decided to have Joseph put in jail since he refused to fall for the temptation of her seduction. She lied about it, and he went to jail. So now he's experiencing adversity again. What happens in the jail? God gave him success. What is Joseph doing in the middle of this adversity? Living in the Covenant. He still believes. He says, *I still trust, believe, and understand the authority of God that in the middle of this problem, God can give me favor and Covenant, and I can live out a grand life.* Wow. This is the attitude he had while he was living in jail. He easily could have gone the opposite direction, going right to the flesh and feeling sorry for himself. Woe is me. Why is this happening? Why is God doing this to me? I'm just going to sit here and be miserable because I guess that's my lot in life.

Then Pharaoh has a dream about a famine. He doesn't understand it. What happens? The chief cupbearer remembers that while he was in jail, Joseph had interpreted his dream and informs Pharaoh. Joseph then gives his interpretation of Pharaoh's dream, which Pharaoh found acceptable and accurate and decides to release Joseph from jail and put him in the position of second in command for the entire kingdom. This is an example of extreme Covenant favor from God. We know the end of the story. What ultimately happened? They had a famine and Joseph's wisdom from God and leadership saved Egypt—and Israel. He was blessed to be a blessing—exercising the authority of God. We are to remember we have authority from God—to ask Him for favor in the middle of difficulties. And God will provide this favor and complete resolution, including His freedom and joy.

What does it mean to be a good and faithful servant? How does this translate into experiencing God's authority and blessing? How are we then to respond to God's assignments? Why?

> **Read Matthew 25:15–23:**
>
> [15] To one he gave five talents,[a] to another two, to another one, to each according to his ability. Then he went away. [16] He who had received the five talents went at once and traded with them, and he made five talents more. [17] So also he who had the two talents made two talents more. [18] But he who had received the one talent went and dug in the ground and hid his master's money. [19] Now after a long time the master of those servants came and settled accounts with them. [20] And he who had received the five talents came forward, bringing five talents more, saying, 'Master, you delivered to me five talents; here, I have made five talents more.' [21] His master said to him, 'Well done, good and faithful servant.[b] You have been faithful over a little; I will set you over much. Enter into the joy of your master.' [22] And he also who had the two talents came forward, saying, 'Master, you delivered to me two talents; here, I have made two talents more.' [23] His master said to him, 'Well done, good and faithful servant. You have been faithful over a little; I will set you over much. Enter into the joy of your master.'

____

____

____

____

____

The reward for the servant who received five talents and the reward for the servant who received two talents was what? The same thing. It's not about bigness. It's not about working to get Him more. It's not about the outcome. It's about doing well and being a good and faithful servant.

LESSON 3:
WHAT IS IT WE ARE TO EXPECT AS WE EXPERIENCE GOD'S AUTHORITY AND SUPERNATURAL WORKS IN OUR PERSONAL LIVES?

Ephesians 2:10 says that God has prepared for us in advance what He calls good for His purposes, His Kingdom work—and we are to walk in this good by joining God in His good. We are on His path, and we're experiencing His covenant life because we are faithful—joining Him in His work of good. We carry out the assignment of exercising the authority that He's given to us. Well done. We've walked into His works, which is why we are never to judge or question these assignments. Good and faithful servant. Faithful to what? Joining what He's called us to be part of by exercising the authority He has given us. Apart from Him, we're doing what? Nothing. Everything we're doing, quite frankly, is nothing because it's not fulfilling what He has planned for us. Well done. Good and faithful servant. We've been faithful to follow Him and exercise His authority in it. God says that because we've been faithful in this assignment that He gave us, we now enter into His what? Joy. In addition to this joy, He will give us greater things. He will give us authority over greater things. It doesn't necessarily mean our assignments will be bigger or that the numbers will get bigger. Rather, that He will show us more in the next thing.

What limits God's authority in our lives? Why? What then shall be our response when He is desiring to do supernatural things in our lives?

> **Read Mark 6:5–6:**
>
> [5] And he could do no mighty work there, except that he laid his hands on a few sick people and healed them. [6] And he marveled because of their unbelief.
>
> And he went about among the villages teaching.

____

____

____

____

____

Jesus came to do these supernatural things through His authority, and the people said, *We're not willing to be persuaded that what You have to say is true. We reject this.* So, He marveled. The word *marveled* means He was dumbfounded. He said, *I don't get that. How is it possible that I'm here to do this and you're limiting Me? I can't fulfill it through your lack of willingness to believe—to join Me in My authority.* So we have limited things that will happen because we're struggling between our own desires and living in faith. Remember, He is the author and finisher of faith. We are not to get stuck in doubt, which ultimately limits God.

How do we not neglect so great a salvation in God bearing witness to His life by supernatural works? What then is important for us to believe, receive, and exercise in our lives?

Read Hebrews 2:1–4:

Warning Against Neglecting Salvation

2 Therefore we must pay much closer attention to what we have heard, lest we drift away from it. [2] For since the message declared by angels proved to be reliable, and every transgression or disobedience received a just retribution, [3] how shall we escape if we neglect such a great salvation? It was declared at first by the Lord, and it was attested to us by those who heard, [4] while God also bore witness by signs and wonders and various miracles and by gifts of the Holy Spirit distributed according to his will.

God says that our life is to become whole through His work, day after day, week after week, month after month. God says He will bear witness to that life by doing what? Signs and wonders, miracles, gifts of the Holy Spirit, according to His will. He's saying that we can be assured that if we're walking with Him, we will experience and offer to others to experience the supernatural. Where does that come from? Authority. Why? Because He speaks, which is superior to the material to any circumstance we might have. Because we're living in a natural world that's under the control of the enemy, we will have difficulty, have trouble. But don't worry, He has overcome it. He can resolve these things by speaking to them and changing them. That's why He says this in both the Old Testament and the New Testament numerous times. Is there anything too difficult for Him? What's the answer? No. Why not? All He has to do is speak because He's superior to it. Spiritually, in the Kingdom of God, He is superior—He has the power over the kingdom of the enemy, in which we happen to be living. But while we're living in this place, He says, *If I were you, as I have set before you life or death, choose to live in the Kingdom of God.* This is where the authority is given and exercised. What does that look like? Surrendering our will, letting Him be King, and then letting Him speak to our circumstance—we receive it, and we exercise that given authority; and start to see restoration and resolution. This is conditional on our surrender—as Christ had go to Gethsemane and had to surrender His will. He had to struggle through His battle of the will until He finally got to the third time and said: *I truly have surrendered My will. I'd rather have You do it differently, but I'm following You because Your will is best and none better.*

On what basis can we be assured that all of the followers of Christ are to experience His supernatural promises in our lives? Why? What is the condition to us receiving these, and why can we not just choose our own promises?

Read 2 Corinthians 1:18–24:

[18] As surely as God is faithful, our word to you has not been Yes and No. [19] For the Son of God, Jesus Christ, whom we proclaimed among you, Silvanus and Timothy and I, was not Yes and No, but in him it is always Yes. [20] For all the promises of God find their Yes in him. That is why it is through him that we utter our Amen to God for his glory. [21] And it is God who establishes us with you in Christ, and has anointed us, [22] and who has also put his seal on us and given us his Spirit in our hearts as a guarantee.[a]

[23] But I call God to witness against me—it was to spare you that I refrained from coming again to Corinth. [24] Not that we lord it over your faith, but we work with you for your joy, for you stand firm in your faith.

____

____

____

____

____

In verse 1:24 Paul says he doesn't have authority over our faith, over our choices because of what? Free will. Paul does say that he is going to exercise authority as God has spoken to him. But the one thing he needs to help us understand is that we don't have the authority to alter our will so that he can fulfill what he believes is a resolution. Why not? Because God doesn't and we can't step in where He doesn't go. We have authority over things, over events, over sickness and disease because anything that the enemy has, He has authority over. He says the key is that all the promises are what? Yes, and amen. We are to say we've received the promise. We've heard His voice. We are going to exercise that authority through belief. The word amen means: may it be, so may it be fulfilled. For what? What He spoke to us—His promises, which in Scripture total more than 7,000—is yes. So, they are all yes, and there's no arbitration to that. All of them are yes. To whom? Everybody, all of His children. Come be with Him. By definition, this is why we're in the Kingdom, where all the promises are yes. When we have problems, what should we do? Ask Him what He has to say. _God, what do You have to speak? What promise are You giving us for this situation?_ Because He knows something—it's going to be yes, because it's in Christ. We can't go decide on our own that we want a particular one. That's called name it and claim it, which is worthless because it's an example of using our self-will to try to grab it, and so by definition, we're out of the Kingdom. We're not following Him, we're following self—trying to determine our own solution—even using His promises, which are available but not spoken to us. Rather, we are to ask Him what He has to say. He assures us that He will speak. _This is My promise to you. Now walk with Me into that promise._ He is going to give us Covenant.

What is important for us to process together His mighty work in our lives, especially when we are dealing with difficult people who are a struggle for us?

Read Ephesians 4:24–29:

[24] and to put on the new self, created after the likeness of God in true righteousness and holiness.

[25] Therefore, having put away falsehood, let each one of you speak the truth with his neighbor, for we are members one of another. [26] Be angry and do not sin; do not let the sun go down on your anger, [27] and give no opportunity to the devil. [28] Let the thief no longer steal, but rather let him labor, doing honest work with his own hands, so that he may have something to share with anyone in need. [29] Let no corrupting talk come out of your mouths, but only such as is good for building up, as fits the occasion, that it may give grace to those who hear.

____

____

____

____

____

We put on the new creation, given to us in the likeness of God—true righteousness and holiness. We are to put on the life of Christ in the Kingdom, where we have the power, the authority of Christ. We do this by coming to truth, letting no unwholesome talk come from our discussions—only what is going to be effective. When we have a problem, what's effective? Hearing from the Lord and speaking, believing, and encouraging each other with what God spoke. We go to a place where we get clarity. Since we understand it now, we can exercise it and join together in that process where we expect God to fulfill His word of authority with clarity (unity).

What is the prophetic, and what role does this play in experiencing God's authority and helping others experience God's authority? Why?

> **Read 1 Corinthians 14:1–3:**
>
> Prophecy and Tongues
> **14** Pursue love, and earnestly desire the spiritual gifts, especially that you may prophesy. [2] For one who speaks in a tongue speaks not to men but to God; for no one understands him, but he utters mysteries in the Spirit. [3] On the other hand, the one who prophesies speaks to people for their upbuilding and encouragement and consolation.

____

____

____

____

____

With the prophetic, we speak to each other the words and the promises we personally hear from God. We are fore tellers and a forth tellers (truth tellers). We can be the messengers of God (and also recipients when others are messengers to us). We then process that together to get to unity, to clarity of God's will. That's where the authority is. Together, we can go to the process of understanding and believing God's will.

As we experience God's authority, how do we continue to abide in Him, and why is it so important to receive what God has to say from Him and not rely on others? Why?

> **Read 1 John 2:24–27:**
>
> [24] Let what you heard from the beginning abide in you. If what you heard from the beginning abides in you, then you too will abide in the Son and in the Father. [25] And this is the promise that he made to us[a]—eternal life.
> [26] I write these things to you about those who are trying to deceive you. [27] But the anointing that you received from him abides in you, and you have no need that anyone should teach you. But as his anointing teaches you about everything, and is true, and is no lie—just as it has taught you, abide in him.

____

____

____

____

____

He says that we don't have need for anybody else to teach us because He is the giver of the authority, the giver of the truth that resides in Him. Therefore, we should always make sure we're hearing from Him. Don't let anybody else ever tell us differently. We need to hear directly from God and then have other's join to confirm what we are hearing. Do not fall victim to laziness, asking others what should be done. We have the teacher within us. We don't need anybody else to teach us per se—we just need to walk with others to help confirm it. Continue to abide and walk forward in the truth already revealed—God's will is a step-by-step process and the path is based upon the truth already known. Do not backtrack and start over when something comes before us—instead, evaluate this new "something" to determine if it lines up with what we have already understood as truth—how God walks us forward into His supernatural work.

A simple example: A senior executive was looking for work, and he and his wife had heard from God: *Your new CEO job will be where you only travel two nights every other week because you have young kids and a young wife. I'll give you that job as part of My Covenant promise that your life will be grand for you, your wife, and your kids.*

Guess what comes along? A new job that pays twice as much money as he's ever made in his life, traveling five nights a week, every week. He starts to think that this opportunity might be God's will. Why? Because he rationalizes that there is so much he can do with all this extra money—like support the church.

God told him and his wife that the new job would only require two nights of travel every other week, but this job required five nights every week. He already knew what the truth was, and he needed to go forward with the truth, not backtrack just because there was more money involved. He turned down the position and two weeks later received a job offer from a fantastic company for a fantastic role that required only two nights' travel every other week and also paid twice as much money as he'd ever made before in his life. It was clear that was better. That was good. Follow the truth of God and receive His best and none better.

From the following three sets of verses, why is it important for us to hear what He has to say? To believe what He has to say? Then pray what He has to say so that we experience His authority of supernatural works in our lives.

Read John 14:12–14:

[12] "Truly, truly, I say to you, whoever believes in me will also do the works that I do; and greater works than these will he do, because I am going to the Father. [13] Whatever you ask in my name, this I will do, that the Father may be glorified in the Son. [14] If you ask me[a] anything in my name, I will do it.

____

____

____

____

____

We need to ask Him, *What is Your will? What authority do You give us?* It is similar to how a company works. The CEO of a company reports to a board of directors. The authority rests there. CEOs can't make unilateral decisions without the approval of the board of directors. CEOs can't just write checks to purchase other companies. The money is not theirs personally, and they don't have the authority to perform transactions of that nature. Once the board of directors authorizes the transaction, the CEO can move forward with the execution of it. How would he do this? He uses the board of director's authority. God says that we can't move forward on our own unless we hear what He has to say, giving us the authority—in His name, because He has the power to execute it through us.

Read John 15:7–8:

[7] If you abide in me, and my words abide in you, ask whatever you wish, and it will be done for you. [8] By this my Father is glorified, that you bear much fruit and so prove to be my disciples.

We're abiding in the relationship in the Kingdom and have surrendered our will. We're walking with Him. And now His words abide in us. What have we done? We've heard what He's said, and we believe it. When we get to that point, we can now ask the Father to perform what He just said. It will be done and by this, glorify Him. What will glorify the Father? Supernatural work. We couldn't have done it in the natural, so we can't take credit for it. Rather, we're excited to say, *Look at what God did!* He wants us to tell the whole story. We abided with Him. We heard His voice. We processed to the point where we believed it. We started praying it, and He did it. Don't just tell the end of the story where God did what He did. If we tell the whole story, it is far more likely that people will wonder if that is possible for them, too. Through the telling of the whole story, others can learn to abide and experience the supernatural work of God.

LESSON 3:
WHAT IS IT WE ARE TO EXPECT AS WE EXPERIENCE GOD'S AUTHORITY AND SUPERNATURAL WORKS IN OUR PERSONAL LIVES?

Read 1 John 5:14–15:

14 And this is the confidence that we have toward him, that if we ask anything according to his will he hears us. 15 And if we know that he hears us in whatever we ask, we know that we have the requests that we have asked of him.

If we ask according to His will, we must have heard and received what God speaks to us about the situation—it is His will. If we are going to pray according to His will, what must He do? Tell us or show us His will. He will speak His will. We'll hear it, and He will confirm it. Ask others who are close to us to confirm it. If we don't quite understand it or we are confused, what is He going to do? He will continue to reveal His will. He'll help us a little bit farther. He will send somebody to help reveal this more. He will have something happen that will help us understand His will so we can have clarity and pray it. Then, it'll happen. Pray now according to His will, and it will be received.

LESSON 3:
WHAT IS IT WE ARE TO EXPECT AS WE EXPERIENCE GOD'S AUTHORITY AND SUPERNATURAL WORKS IN OUR PERSONAL LIVES?

As we hear, receive, believe His promises, and recognize His authority, what is important for us as we are a participant in exercising this authority? What are we to see and then speak? Why is this so important?

Read Mark 11:20–25:

The Lesson from the Withered Fig Tree

[20] As they passed by in the morning, they saw the fig tree withered away to its roots. [21] And Peter remembered and said to him, "Rabbi, look! The fig tree that you cursed has withered." [22] And Jesus answered them, "Have faith in God. [23] Truly, I say to you, whoever says to this mountain, 'Be taken up and thrown into the sea,' and does not doubt in his heart, but believes that what he says will come to pass, it will be done for him. [24] Therefore I tell you, whatever you ask in prayer, believe that you have received[a] it, and it will be yours. [25] And whenever you stand praying, forgive, if you have anything against anyone, so that your Father also who is in heaven may forgive you your trespasses."[b]

____

____

____

____

____

On Palm Sunday, Jesus was walking through Jerusalem when He sees this fig tree and curses it. He and the disciples were walking back out the next day on their way to Bethany to see Mary, Martha, and Lazarus. As they are walking toward the fig tree, He's waiting. Do you notice anything? Are you paying attention? Did you see something? And Peter did notice and said, _That tree that you cursed is completely withered. It's gone._ Since Peter noticed this, Jesus explained that it all happens by Him speaking, but they will also get to that same place. Have faith in God, or rather, have the faith OF God. What does He have to say? Have His faith, which He will give us. We've got to hear and believe. Once we do, what then? Speak to the mountain—knowing that moving it seems impossible. He says to speak to it. Yes, there's a risk. Are we willing publicly to speak what He just said? What if it doesn't happen? Then we didn't believe it, but we are to keep going until we can speak it. He didn't say that we are to pray that He grants our desired outcome and resolution. Rather, what are we going to do? We are to take the word and apply it to that situation. We need to go and lay hands on that person to get healed. We speak to it. If we have a business problem, we ask the Father what He has to say about it, what resolution, promise is His will, under His authority? We then speak this very word to what? Our issue. Don't just ask God to do something, rather we need to speak to the issue. And He said that when we do that, it's going to happen.

Verse 24 summarizes this. When we speak what we have heard in faith, believe it has already happened, and it will happen. Past tense. God is not limited by time—what does He see? It's already done. We need to join Him in that. He wants us to believe that we see it already being done and now we can pray it, declare it, speak it. When will it be done? In the future. We see it already done like He does, and now we can experience the supernatural by exercising the authority and joining in and being an active participant. He says the works are being done by us because of His authority, which is now being exercised through us. He's not bypassing us—just asking us to hear, believe, and speak.

To confirm His will and His desire to fulfill authority and supernatural in our lives, what beautiful way has He given for us to have complete confidence? How does this work? Why is this so important?

Read Matthew 18:18–20:

[18] Truly, I say to you, whatever you bind on earth shall be bound in heaven, and whatever you loose on earth shall be loosed[a] in heaven. [19] Again I say to you, if two of you agree on earth about anything they ask, it will be done for them by my Father in heaven. [20] For where two or three are gathered in my name, there am I among them."

____

____

____

____

____

We are to gather in His name, hear what He speaks and go to unity in the Spirit with two or more. Get to unity when we then can bind up the work of the enemy and loose the power of heaven into our situations. Who's doing that? We are. We don't need to ask God to take care of our situations. No, we are doing it where? In the Kingdom where the power is, flowing through us, as we receive and believe in unity that He spoke—the source of the authority.

As we summarize, we are able to do this because:

1. We put on the new creation, after the likeness of God in true righteousness and holiness.

2. Having put away falsehood, we each speak the truth with those who are seeking God's will.

3. We are members, so we are to build each other up with walking together into the supernatural, exercising His authority that He is giving to us to hear, believe, and speak.

We are to put on the life of Christ in the Kingdom; live out the power authority of Christ, for the purpose of assisting each other, coming to truth, and being effective in experiencing His supernatural work. It's all about the authority. While we are following Him, we're going to have issues because we live in a difficult, troublesome world. We're going to have decisions, issues, and things that aren't working—problems. We are to ask God what He has to say about those. He will speak to it. We will hear it. He will then confirm it. Do we believe it so that we can speak it ahead of time? When we see that happen, we're going to experience the supernatural all the time.